Please Read this First

This book is a bridge to your new life!

Do not allow the brevity of each page or the simplicity of the words cause you to treat the use of this book lightly.

This book is designed to help you save and improve your marriage by way of using text messages.

If you desire to improve your marriage, this notebook was designed specifically for you.

No matter what level of disconnection and pain your marital relationship is currently experiencing, your marriage can be saved, improved and be a happy one.

This book uses a simple principle and strategy that will help you reconnect and save or improve your marriage.

The **PRINCIPLE:** Treat a man as his actions deserve, and he will remain as he is – Treat a man as he ought to behave, and he will rise the standard.

And what does this mean? Well, if your husband is behaving like an idiot and you respond by treating him like an idiot, he will remain behaving like an idiot. On the other hand, if your husband is behaving like an idiot and you treat him like a King, he will rise his standard and become a king.

The **STRATEGY:** Send honoring and affirming text messages to him everyday at the same time for the next 30 days.

Why These Text Messages?

Respect is to your husband what love is to you. His crave for respect is equal your need for love. This text message strategy has been used and proven efficient since the year 2012.

How it Really Works:
Send your text messages everyday (six days per week) at the same time, preferably in the mornings. 8:30am and 9am have proven to be every effective for most people.

And What if He Responds? When he responds, respond back. If he asks why you are sending the messages, answer "because it is true", or do not respond at all.

And What If The Text Message Is Completely The Opposite Of His Character? Good question. If for example, the text message of the day says "You are an honest men", but in reality, he is a liar, the strategy is to treat a man as he ought to behave and he will rise to the standard. He may in fact be a liar, and your strategy is to help him be the honest man.

Do Not send more than one text message per day. This does not mean that you should not communicate about other things. It just means this intervention strategy should be separate from you other everyday business.

9 Things You Should NOT Do During this Phase

1. No matter how much hurt you are, do not ever send him angry text messages.
2. Do not apologize over text message.
3. If you are facing divorce or he has left, do not apologize yet. You can do so in person after you have seen that the two of you are reconnecting. Only after the first 30 days of you sending the text messages.
4. If he is cheating or living with someone else, do not send your text message when he might be with the person that he is cheating on you with.
5. For the first two weeks, do not send more than one text message per day. Two will be okay, but do not flood him with your messages. Putting pressure on him may cause him to back-off from you more.
6. Most probably on or by the 3rd day, he will call you and ask you what's going on or why you are sending these messages. If he asks you why, you could say; "because it is true". Do not say "I finally realize how much I love you" or anything that has a negative connotation.
7. If he has left, do not ask him to come back. You can do that later, just not now. Do not ask questions like, "Why did you leave? What did I do wrong?" Such questions have negative connotations and tend to also bring emotional pressure on the other. Rather ask questions like: Did you know you are the greatest lover?
8. Do not talk about forgiveness yet. The strategy is to reconnect with your husbands heart through what he was designed to crave the most – RESPECT.
9. During the next thirty one days, DO NOT ask your husband for anything. This is strictly a time of building up, stirring up and fixing your relationship.

How it Works

1. Decide on what time of the day you will send your text messages. It is important that you send you text messages at the same time everyday.

2. Communicate your message (via text message only). The strategy in this book has worked very well with text messages, and we do not yet know how much effective other avenues are.

3. After sending your message, write your present moment thoughts, and feelings.

4. Use this book as your diary: Write down any responses you receive, lessons learned, any other experiences you might have gone through and anything you deem important.

5. If it helps, discuss with your friends about your activities, however, please watch out for negative friends, especially the ones that always find something negative to say about him. I strongly suggest that you stay away from friends of the opposite sex unless they are family.

6. When you send your text messages, send them as they are written in this book. Do not add a 'period' or full stop at the end of the message. Trust me, it makes a huge difference.

7. Extra help for those who desire to save and improve their marriage is available at TovNation@Gmail.com. Please only seek extra help after you have used this book for at least 10 days.

Let's Get Started...

I love you

I love you more everyday

You're simply the best

I'm thinking about you right now

What would you like me to wear to bed tonight? I hope you say nothing

You are a man of honor

I love you

You and I, naked sweaty and moaning. Got anything
to add to that?

Just thinking about you makes me feel good

I wouldn't mind giving you head tonight

I'm one lucky woman because I have you

I have loads of respect for you

I love you

On the agenda for tonight: me on top of you

You're one of the most interesting people I've ever met

I'm so grateful to have you in my life

I'm thinking of you

I hope you are having a great day

I'm constantly reminded everyday why I fell in love
with you. Thank you

I love you

I'm so thankful that we fell in love with each other

Good morning beautiful

I'm so thankful that we met

Thinking about your smile

I love our life together

I love you

Just smiling and thinking of you

You smell really good

I love you

You make me feel so good

Well done for completing 30 days of loving and reconnecting with your husband.

How is it going for you? Is this strategy working well for you? If yes, please feel free continue loving and reconnecting with him. Nothing beats intimate connection between spouses!

If you have done everything by the book and not much improvement has come your way, and you could do with extra help, contact TovNation@Gmail.com immediately.

My desire is to help you save and improve your marriage.

I appreciate you so much

I love being with you

I love you

I look up to you

Thanks for being you

You're the best person

I love us

Thanks for being a great husband

I'm glad you're my friend

I love you

You're a great husband

I really appreciate you

You are awesome

I respect you so much

Thanks for working so hard

You're an excellent provider

I love you

You're so smart

You're amazing

You're so strong

You're a hard worker

I feel safe with you

I like you

I love you

You're so considerate

You're a great lover

I'll go wherever you lead

I'm blessed you are my husband

You are a godly man

Thank you for leading our family

Well done for completing 60 days of loving and reconnecting with your husband.

How is it going for you? Is this strategy working well for you? If yes, please feel free continue loving and reconnecting with him. Nothing beats intimate connection between spouses!

If you have done everything by the book and not much improvement has come your way, and you could do with extra help, contact TovNation@Gmail.com immediately.

My desire is to help you save and improve your marriage.

I love you

It's fun to be married to you

You are a generous person

You are my favorite person in the entire world!

I want to grow old with you

You're trustworthy

I trust your judgment

I love you

You are a thoughtful man

I have confidence in you

I totally trust you

I'm proud to be your wife

There's no one like you

You stand for the truth. I admire that

I love you

You are a man of conviction

You are a man of integrity

You're amazing – you really are

You're a man of action

I honor you

There's no one like you

I love you

Thank you for being a faithful husband (and father)

You are so very handsome

The heavens must really be looking out for me to give me you!

You are an excellent role model

You're a gentleman

I love just being with you

I'll love you always and forever

I love you

No matter what level of disconnection and pain your marital relationship is currently experiencing, your marriage can be saved, improved and be a happy one. Extra help for those who desire to save and improve their marriage is available at
TovNation@Gmail.com